**Pearson Education Limited**
Edinburgh Gate, Harlow,
Essex CM20 2JE, England
and Associated Companies throughout the world.

ISBN: 978-1-4058-6238-7

First published by Penguin Books 2005
This edition published 2008

7  9  10  8

Text copyright © Penguin Books Ltd 2005
This edition copyright © Pearson Education Ltd 2008
Illustrations copyright © Maggie Downer 2005

Typeset by Graphicraft Ltd, Hong Kong
Set in 11/14pt Bembo
Printed in China
SWTC/07

For a complete list of the titles available in the Penguin Readers series please write to your local
Pearson Longman office or to: Penguin Readers Marketing Department, Pearson Education,
Edinburgh Gate, Harlow, Essex CM20 2JE, England.

# *Contents*

Contents

# *Introduction*

*'Lovers, crazy people and the writers of poems believe in these silly fairy stories, but I don't.'*

These are the words of Theseus, the Duke of Athens, on his wedding night. He is talking about the story that two pairs of lovers – Lysander and Hermia, Demetrius and Helena – have told him about their night in the wood outside Athens. At the beginning of the story, Lysander and Hermia are in love – but they have a problem. The Duke of Athens tells Hermia that she cannot marry Lysander. She must marry Demetrius – or die! What can Hermia and Lysander do to save their love? They run away into a fairyland wood outside Athens. There Oberon and Titania, the King and Queen of the Fairies, have their own difficult problems to solve . . .

When people see this play, some agree with Theseus. They think that the story of lovers and fairies is silly. But for most people, the story is not the most important thing about the play. The play is about ideas and feelings, love and dreams. People dream when they are asleep. When they fall in love, they also *imagine* things. These things are not real, but they are important. Nobody can see the fairies in the wood. But does that mean that fairies don't exist? The fairies play games with people. They change the lovers' lives. Dreams shape the way that we see the real world. So does it really matter if they are real or not?

William Shakespeare (1564–1616) is the most famous writer of plays in the English language. He was born in Stratford-upon-Avon, in England. He went to a good school, but did not go to university. In 1582, he married Anne Hathaway and had three children. By 1592, he was famous in London as an actor and a writer. Over the next twenty years, he wrote thirty-seven plays and many famous poems. He sometimes wrote three plays a year! His plays were very popular, and many of them were acted in front of King James I. When Shakespeare died in 1616, he was a rich man.

*A Midsummer Night's Dream* (1595) is one of Shakespeare's earlier plays. Most people agree that he wrote it for somebody's wedding. When it was first acted, the same actors usually played Theseus and Oberon, and Hippolyta and Titania.

The title of the play seems strange to the modern reader. We now think of June as the middle of an English summer, but this story happens just before 1 May – May Day. This is because there were only three seasons in Shakespeare's time: autumn, winter and summer. Spring was not a special season – it was a part of the summer. May Day, the middle of summer, was the time of year when animals were put out into the fields. People believed that this was a special time for love and dreams. It was also a time for fairies that brought life and colour to the earth after the hard months of winter.

*A Midsummer Night's Dream* is as popular today as it was 400 years ago. It has some of Shakespeare's most beautiful language. It has given us two of his funniest and most famous people: Puck, the likeable but childish fairy, and Bottom, the silly actor with the donkey's head. There have been many films of *A Midsummer Night's Dream*. The most famous one was a Hollywood film in 1936, with James Cagney as Bottom. In 1999, Hollywood made another film of the play, with Kevin Kline as Bottom and Michelle Pfeiffer as Titania.

The play is also important for one more reason: it gave the world the idea of fairies! It was the first work of literature that showed fairies as small flying creatures, like little people. Children's writers and Disney films still use the same idea today.

# Reading and acting the play

You can read *A Midsummer Night's Dream* silently, like every other story in a book. You will have to imagine the places, the people's clothes and their voices from the words on the page.

But Shakespeare did not write *A Midsummer Night's Dream* as literature for reading. He wrote it for actors on a theatre stage. You can read the play in a group with other people. This is very different from silent reading. You can speak the words and bring the people in the play to life. They can sound happy or sad, worried or angry. You can add silences and important noises, like the sound of music. You can also stop and discuss the play. What does this person mean? Why do they say that?

But you can have more fun if you act the play. *A Midsummer Night's Dream* has a lot of movement and colour. There are many funny scenes and conversations. There are poems, music and dancing, too. The people in the play have to show a lot of different feelings. In the funniest parts, their feelings change very quickly. If you act the play, you can show these feelings by your words *and* actions.

The scenes should look different – a palace in Athens, a market square, a dark forest at night. You should think about special clothes for the fairies, the young lovers, the poor workers from the market, and the Duke and his courtiers. You should also think about stage equipment – swords, lanterns, and a donkey's head for Bottom! *A Midsummer Night's Dream* has a lot of people in it. You should think about how to make the fairies different from the 'real' people. Remember – the people in the play cannot see the fairies, but the audience can! Some people in the play don't speak, but their actions on stage are important. How many fairies do you need? How many guests will there be at Theseus's wedding party?

*A Midsummer Night's Dream* is a wonderful play. You can read it or act it. But have fun and enjoy it!

# The People in the Play

THESEUS, Duke of Athens
HIPPOLYTA, Queen of the Amazons, Theseus's future wife
PHILOSTRATE, Theseus's chief assistant
EGEUS, Hermia's father
HERMIA, Egeus's daughter, in love with Lysander
LYSANDER, in love with Hermia
DEMETRIUS, in love with Hermia
HELENA, in love with Demetrius
OTHER LORDS, friends and courtiers of Theseus

QUINCE, a furniture-maker
SNUG, a bread-maker
BOTTOM, a cloth-maker
FLUTE, a shoe-mender
SNOUT, a tool-mender
STARVELING, a shirt-maker

OBERON, King of the Fairies
TITANIA, Queen of the Fairies
PUCK, a fairy, Oberon's messenger
PEASEBLOSSOM, a fairy, Titania's courtier
COBWEB, a fairy, Titania's courtier
MUSTARDSEED, a fairy, Titania's courtier
OTHER FAIRIES, courtiers to Oberon and Titania

## Act 1   Lovers and Actors

*Scene 1   A room in Theseus's palace*

[*Theseus, Hippolyta and Philostrate arrive.*]

THESEUS: In four days' time, there will be a new moon and we
will be married. But oh, how slow this old moon is!
HIPPOLYTA [*smiling*]: If you keep busy, the time will soon pass.
THESEUS: You are right. Philostrate, go and prepare the young
people of the city for four days of fun and parties. There will be
no sadness in Athens on our wedding night. [*Philostrate leaves.*]
Hippolyta, it was not easy to win your love. I had to fight other
men away with my sword. You were unhappy then, I know. But
I promise you that now I will bring you only happiness.

[*Egeus arrives with Hermia, Lysander and Demetrius.*]

EGEUS: I hope you will be very happy, my Lord.
THESEUS: Thank you, Egeus. What is your news?
EGEUS: I have a problem with my daughter, Hermia. [*pointing to
Demetrius*] This man has my permission to marry her. But
[*pointing to Lysander*] *this* is the man that she loves! [*turning to
Lysander*] Yes, you, Lysander! You have given my daughter
gifts, sung at her window by moonlight, and now you have
stolen her heart! You have turned her against me, her own
father. [*turning to Theseus*] She is mine. I have the power to
choose a husband for her. And I have chosen Demetrius. But
if she refuses to listen to me, I can also send her to her death.
That is an old Athenian law. My Lord, do I have your
permission to use the law?
THESEUS: Hermia, your father gave you life and happiness. And
now he has the power to take them away. If you are wise, you
will marry Demetrius. He is a good man.

1

HERMIA: Lysander is a good man, too!

THESEUS: Yes, I am sure that he is. But in your father's opinion, Demetrius will be a better husband.

HERMIA: Why can't my father see things through my eyes?

THESEUS: Why can't *you* see things through *his*?

HERMIA: My Lord, please forgive me, but the power of love is so strong. I cannot understand it, but I cannot escape from it either. What will happen to me if I refuse to marry Demetrius?

THESEUS: You must promise to live away from the world of men, in a place of religion, for the rest of your life. If you cannot promise that, you will have to die. Think about it, Hermia. Is it right for a beautiful girl like you to spend all her life alone in cold, empty rooms?

HERMIA: I would prefer to do that than to marry Demetrius.

THESEUS: I will give you four days to think about it, Hermia. Then, if you still refuse to marry Demetrius, you must prepare yourself for a life of loneliness – or death!

DEMETRIUS: Think again, sweet Hermia. And you, Lysander, stop this crazy game. Hermia is mine.

LYSANDER: You have her father's love, Demetrius. Why can't I have Hermia's?

EGEUS: Yes, he has my love, and I have decided to give him my daughter as his wife.

LYSANDER: But my Lord, I am as good as Demetrius, if not better. I love her more than he does. She loves me, not him! Can't you see that love is just a game to Demetrius? A short time ago he won the heart of Nedar's daughter, Helena, and she still loves him. How can you believe that your daughter will be safe with a dishonest man like him?

THESEUS: It is true – I have heard about Demetrius and Helena. I wanted to talk to Demetrius about it earlier, but I forgot. Come with me, Demetrius – and you, too, Egeus. You can

2

help me prepare for my wedding. While we are doing that, we can discuss a few things. And you, fair Hermia, listen to your father, or the law of Athens will punish you!

[*Egeus, Hippolyta, Demetrius and Theseus leave.*]

LYSANDER: What's the matter, my love? Why is your face so pale?

HERMIA: I'm not free to marry you. How can I be happy?

LYSANDER: We must be brave. True love has never been an easy journey.

HERMIA: You mean that our problems are not unusual?

LYSANDER: I mean exactly that. And if we're brave and patient, we'll find happiness together.

HERMIA: How?

LYSANDER: A long way from Athens, I have an aunt who has no husband or children. She thinks of me as her only son. We can marry there, because the law of Athens can't reach us. If you love me, run away from your father's house tomorrow night. Meet me in the palace wood where I saw you and Helena picking flowers one day last May.

HERMIA: I promise you with all my heart that I'll be there.

LYSANDER: I'll see you tomorrow, then . . . But look! Here comes Helena.

[*Helena arrives, looking pale and unhappy.*]

HERMIA: Fair Helena, how good it is to see you.

HELENA: Don't call me 'fair', because it isn't true. *You're* the fair one. Demetrius loves *you*. Your eyes are like stars and your voice is as sweet as a bird's song. Teach me how to be like you. Tell me your secret. How did you succeed in stealing Demetrius's heart?

HERMIA: I look coldly at him, but he still loves me.

HELENA: Oh, why can't my smiles be as beautiful as your cold eyes?

3

HERMIA: I'm rude to him, but he still gives me love.

HELENA: Why can't he love my kindness?

HERMIA: I show him hate, but he still follows me.

HELENA: I show him love, but he still hates me.

HERMIA: But I've never wanted him to love me.

HELENA: You only have to look at him with your beautiful face.

HERMIA: I promise you, Helena, that Demetrius will not see my face again. Lysander and I have a secret plan. Before I met him, Athens was a wonderful place. But now it's become a bad dream for us. We can't stay here.

HELENA: What are you planning to do?

LYSANDER: Tomorrow night, when the moon paints the dark, sleeping city silver with its light, Hermia and I are going to leave through the gates of Athens.

HERMIA: We're going to meet in the wood where you and I often picked flowers. Then Lysander and I will turn our backs on Athens for ever and start a new life together in another land. So goodbye, my sweet friend, and think of us. I hope with all my heart that Demetrius will soon return your love for him. Now we must go. Goodbye again.

LYSANDER: And good luck with Demetrius.

[*Hermia and Lysander leave.*]

HELENA: How lucky some people are! Everyone in Athens thinks that I'm as beautiful as Hermia – everyone except Demetrius! He loved me until he met Hermia. Then his love for me was forgotten and he only had eyes for her. But I have an idea. If I tell Demetrius about her escape plan, he'll follow her to the wood tomorrow night. When he sees her with Lysander, his eyes will open. Then he'll understand that he'll only ever find true love with me! [*She leaves.*]

'Lysander and I will turn our backs on Athens for ever . . .'

## Scene 2    *A market square in Athens*

[*Quince arrives with Snug, Bottom, Flute, Snout and Starveling.*]

QUINCE: Is everybody here?

BOTTOM: Why don't you check the list? Then you'll know.

QUINCE: I've got the list here.

BOTTOM: Good. First, tell us all about the play that we're going to do for the Duke and Duchess on their wedding night.

QUINCE: It's about the sad, cruel death of Pyramus and Thisby.

BOTTOM: That sounds like a very good play. Now, good Peter Quince, read the actors' names from your list.

QUINCE: Answer as I call you. Nick Bottom, the cloth-maker.

BOTTOM: I'm ready. Who am I going to be?

QUINCE: You're going to be Pyramus.

BOTTOM: What is Pyramus? A lover or a murderer?

QUINCE: A lover who kills himself for love.

BOTTOM: Ah, *that* will make the audience cry! When they see me, they'll cry an ocean of tears! Now, who are the other actors?

QUINCE: Francis Flute the shoe-mender, you'll be Thisby.

FLUTE: Who is Thisby? A brave, handsome soldier?

QUINCE: No, she's the lady that Pyramus loves.

FLUTE: Me, a woman? I can't do that! I'm growing a beard!

QUINCE: That's no problem. You can cover your face and speak in a high voice.

BOTTOM: No, *I'll* play Thisby. I can speak in a *very* high voice. Listen . . .

QUINCE: No, no, you must play Pyramus, and Flute, you'll be Thisby. Robin Starveling, the shirt-maker?

STARVELING: Here, Peter Quince.

QUINCE: You must play Thisby's mother. Tom Snout, the tool-mender? You'll be Pyramus's father. I'll be Thisby's father. Snug, the bread-maker, you're going to be the lion.

6

SNUG: I hope there aren't too many words. I'm a very slow learner.

QUINCE: Don't worry – you just have to roar.

BOTTOM: I'll be the lion, too. I'll roar very loudly and the Duke will say, 'I want to hear that roar again!'

QUINCE: No, you'll frighten the ladies with *your* roar, and then the Duke will kill us all!

BOTTOM: Then I'll roar as sweetly as a bird.

QUINCE: I've already told you, Nick Bottom, you must play Pyramus!

BOTTOM: All right. But what kind of beard shall I have?

QUINCE: You can choose: black, grey, orange, blue or even no beard at all. Now, gentlemen, here are your lines. Learn them well and meet me tomorrow night in the palace wood, outside the city. We can practise our play in secret there by moonlight, and no one will see us. Does everyone understand?

BOTTOM: Don't worry, Peter Quince. We'll be there, and we'll know all our lines perfectly. Until tomorrow night in the palace wood, goodbye.

[*They all leave.*]


# Act 2   The Juice of the Purple Flower

*Scene 1   The palace wood, the next night*

[*A fairy, one of Titania's courtiers, arrives from one side. Puck arrives from the other side.*]

PUCK: Hello, little fairy, what are you doing here?

PEASEBLOSSOM: I'm looking for raindrops for my Fairy Queen. When I find them, I'm going to hang them around the necks of her favourite flowers like little lanterns. But I must hurry, because the Queen and all her fairies will be here soon.

PUCK [*looking worried*]: But the King's having a party here tonight. The Queen mustn't see him. Oberon's angry with her because of a little boy that was stolen from an Indian king. The Queen keeps the child like a pet and puts flowers in his hair, but the King wants the boy to be one of his courtiers. Now the King and Queen never meet. If they meet here tonight, there'll be a terrible fight!

PEASEBLOSSOM: I know who you are. You're Robin Goodfellow, aren't you? The bad little fairy that people call Puck. You're always playing jokes on people and frightening the village girls. But they say that you bring them luck.

PUCK [*smiling proudly*]: Yes, that's me. I am the happy little traveller of the night. Oberon smiles at my funny stories. I tell him about all the jokes that I play ... [*suddenly worried*] But you must go now, quickly! I can hear the King coming.

PEASEBLOSSOM [*nervously*]: Oh, no! My Queen's coming, too! Why does the King have to be here now?

[*Oberon arrives from one side with his fairy courtiers. Titania arrives from the other side with Mustardseed, Cobweb and other fairy courtiers.*]

OBERON: What bad luck to meet you here by moonlight!

TITANIA: Is that you, proud Oberon? Come, fairies, we must leave immediately. I don't want to talk to him.

OBERON: Wait, you impatient woman. Am I not your Lord?

TITANIA: Yes, but I know all about you and your love for Hippolyta, the Queen of the Amazons. Is that why you've come back from India? Because Hippolyta's going to marry Theseus?

OBERON: How can you say that when you love Theseus?

TITANIA [*angrily*]: That's a lie. Your words are like smoke. They hide what's really happening. You've been angry with me for a long time. Since we started fighting, the world has gone crazy. The wind punishes us because we've stopped listening to its music. It pushes dark clouds across the sea and brings us too

8

much rain. The fields are filled with water, so the farmers have stopped working. The paths across the hills are covered with long grass. The air is always cold and wet, so the villagers get ill. The seasons have all changed. Cold mists fall in the middle of summer and spring flowers grow in winter. The world doesn't understand what's happening. It's all because of you!

OBERON: You can stop this war, Titania. If you give me the little Indian boy, we can be happy again.

TITANIA: No, that's impossible, because the boy's mother was my friend. Before the child was born, I sat with her for many hours on sandy beaches by the Indian Ocean. We laughed and talked together, and watched the ships sail away to foreign lands. But she died in childbirth and I promised to look after her child for her. I will not break that promise. I can't give him to you.

OBERON: How long are you going to stay in this wood?

TITANIA: Until after Theseus's wedding day. You can dance with us here in the moonlight if you like. If not, I'll find another place.

OBERON: Give me that boy, and I'll dance with you.

TITANIA: I've told you – that's impossible. Fairies, let's leave. The King and I will only fight if I stay.

[*Titania and her fairies leave.*]

OBERON [*angrily*]: Go away, then. But I'll punish you before you leave this wood. Puck, come here. I want you to do something for me. Do you remember a hill by the sea that you and I sat on a few months ago? We saw Cupid, the love-fairy, flying between the moon and the earth there . . .

PUCK: I remember.

OBERON: Cupid shot an arrow to the ground. It touched a little milk-white flower and turned it purple. Puck, I want you to bring me that flower. When its juice is poured on sleeping eyes, it has strange powers. People fall in love with the next

9

living creature that they see. Bring it to me as quickly as you can.

PUCK: I'll be back in forty minutes! [*He leaves quickly.*]

OBERON [*smiling unpleasantly*]: When Titania falls asleep, I'll put the juice of this flower in her eyes. She'll fall in love with the next creature that she sees – a lion, a sheep or even a donkey! Then I'll offer her something to take away the power of the juice. But only if she gives me the little Indian boy! [*He hears a noise.*] But who's this coming through the trees? I'll hide and listen to their conversation.

[*Oberon and his fairies hide behind a tree. Demetrius arrives. He is followed by Helena.*]

DEMETRIUS [*coldly*]: I don't love you, so stop following me. Where are Lysander and Hermia? Are they really coming to this wood? When I see them, I'll kill one of them. The other is killing *me*. Go away, Helena, and leave me alone!

HELENA [*almost crying*]: I can't leave you, you hard-hearted man. I'll only stop following you if you stop playing with my heart.

DEMETRIUS: How am I playing with your heart? Am I kind to you? Do I say nice things to you? No. I tell you all the time that I don't love you!

HELENA: Yes, and I love you even more. I'm your little dog, Demetrius. You can do anything with me – use me, shout at me, lose me, hit me – but don't stop me following you.

DEMETRIUS: My dislike for you is growing all the time. I feel sick when I look at you!

HELENA: And I feel sick when I *don't* look at *you*!

DEMETRIUS: You're playing a dangerous game, Helena. You've followed a man who doesn't love you into a dark and lonely wood. Who knows what will happen to you?

HELENA: I feel safe with you, Demetrius. When I'm with you, I don't feel alone. You're my world!

DEMETRIUS: I'll run away from you and hide in the wood and leave you to the wild animals.

HELENA: The wildest animal in the forest is not as cruel as you. Run if you want to, but you'll never escape me!

DEMETRIUS: If you follow me, I'll hurt you. Believe me.

HELENA: You hurt me in the town, the country, everywhere, Demetrius. Women aren't as strong as men. We can't fight for love like men do. [*Demetrius leaves.*] I'll follow you. I'm not afraid of anything that happens. If you can't give me love, then give me death! [*She leaves.*]

OBERON [*coming out from behind the tree*]: Don't worry, my poor, unhappy lady. I promise you that things will be all right. Before he leaves the wood tonight, that cruel man will love you. [*Puck comes in.*] Welcome, Puck. Have you got the flower?

PUCK: Yes, here it is.

OBERON: Give it to me. [*taking the flower and smiling*] I know a place where the grass is soft. The smell of wild roses fills the air. Titania often sleeps there when she's tired of dancing. I'll put the juice of this flower in her sleeping eyes and fill her heart with strange and wonderful dreams. And Puck, you must take some of this juice with you. I want you to find a young man who's somewhere in the wood. He'll be easy to find — he's wearing Athenian clothes. A sweet young lady is following him. She's in love with him, but he cruelly refuses her love. You must put the juice in his eyes when he's asleep. But do it carefully. He must see the young lady immediately when he wakes up. With the juice in his eyes, he'll love her even more than she loves him. When you've done that, meet me back here before the first light of morning.

PUCK [*taking some juice from the flower*]: Don't worry, my Lord. I'll do everything that you ask.

[*They leave.*]

11

## Scene 2    *A place in the wood full of flowers*

[*Titania arrives with her fairies.*]

TITANIA: I'm going to rest here. Sing me a song to help me sleep.
FAIRIES: [*singing softly*]: Animals with teeth so sharp,
    Forest birds that wildly scream,
    Dangerous creatures of the dark,
    Don't come near our Fairy Queen.

[*Titania falls asleep and the fairies quietly leave. Oberon arrives. He sees Titania sleeping.*]

OBERON [*putting the juice in Titania's eyes*]: You'll have a big surprise when you wake up. You'll fall in love with the first creature that you see. Will it be a cat, a chicken or a lion? Or even a big, fat, ugly pig? It doesn't matter what it is. The ugliest animal in the world will be the greatest love of your life. Please wake when something terrible is near.

[*Oberon leaves. Lysander and Hermia arrive.*]

LYSANDER: We're both tired, and I've forgotten the way. Let's rest here and wait for daylight.
HERMIA: All right, Lysander. I'm going to rest here on this soft grass. You can find another place to sleep.
LYSANDER: But I want to lie next to you.
HERMIA: No, you mustn't. We're not married yet.
LYSANDER: I promise not to touch you. I just want to feel your heart next to mine.
HERMIA: You know that I want that, too. But we must be patient. It's wrong before we're man and wife. Find another place to sleep, and goodnight, sweet friend.
LYSANDER: Our bodies will sleep in different beds, but my heart will sleep with yours. Until the morning, dear Hermia, goodnight and sleep well.

*'You'll have a big surprise when you wake up.'*

[*Lysander and Hermia sleep. Puck arrives.*]

PUCK: I've travelled all through this forest, but I haven't found anyone from Athens. [*He notices Lysander.*] But wait, who's this? A young man wearing Athenian clothes! [*He notices Hermia.*] And look! The girl's sleeping alone because the man doesn't want to be near her. Well, I'll change all that, you unkind man. [*putting the juice in Lysander's eyes*] This juice in your eyes will destroy the coldness in your heart. When you wake up, you'll give this sweet lady all your love. Her sad, lonely heart will be full of happiness. Now I must return to Oberon.

[*Puck leaves. Demetrius arrives. Helena is running after him.*]

HELENA: You can kill me if you like, sweet Demetrius. But please stop running away from me!

DEMETRIUS: I've told you a hundred times – I don't want you!

HELENA: Please don't leave me alone in this forest.

DEMETRIUS: If you want to stay here, that's *your* problem. I'm going alone! [*He leaves.*]

HELENA: Oh, I'm so tired of running after you. What do I have to do to win your love? Hermia's so lucky with her beautiful eyes. How did her eyes get so bright? Not with salt tears. My eyes are washed with tears more often than hers. No, no, I'm as ugly as a wild pig. Other animals run away from me in fear. It's not surprising that Demetrius runs away from me, too. [*She notices Lysander.*] But who's here? Lysander, on the ground! Is he dead or asleep? I see no blood. Lysander, if you're alive, wake up!

LYSANDER [*waking up*]: Oh, Helena, how beautiful you are! I'll run through fire for one sweet kiss from you, my love! Where's Demetrius? I'll kill him with my sword!

HELENA [*surprised*]: What are you saying, Lysander? You want to kill him just because he loves your Hermia? You know that Hermia loves you! You should be happy.

LYSANDER: Happy with Hermia? I wrongly thought that I loved her. Until last night, my head was full of childish dreams. But now my eyes are filled with your loveliness!

HELENA [*angrily*]: Why are you making fun of me like this? You know how sad I am. Isn't it enough that I can't get a sweet look or a kind word from Demetrius? I thought you were a gentleman. But I was wrong. [*She leaves.*]

LYSANDER [*to himself*]: Luckily, she didn't see Hermia. Hermia, continue sleeping and never come near me again. You're sweet, but too much of a sweet thing makes the stomach sick. Why did I believe that I loved you? I was stupid. But now I can see that Helena is the only girl for me! [*He leaves.*]

HERMIA [*waking up*]: Oh, what a terrible dream! I'm shaking. Lysander, help me! I dreamt that a snake was moving across my skin. It was eating my heart, but you did nothing. You only sat there smiling at me. But where are you, Lysander? Don't frighten me like this. Say something to me, please! [*She leaves.*]

## Act 3   Monsters and Fairies

*Scene 1 · The same part of the wood*

[*Bottom, Quince, Snout, Starveling, Flute and Snug arrive.*]

QUINCE: This is a perfect place for us to practise.

BOTTOM: Peter Quince, there are some things about our play that I don't like. First, the ladies in the audience won't be happy when Pyramus kills himself with his sword.

SNOUT: I agree with you, Nick Bottom.

STARVELING: We must leave it out.

BOTTOM: No, I've got a better idea. Before the play, I'll tell the

15

audience that Pyramus doesn't really kill himself. I'll explain that Pyramus is really me, Nick Bottom. That will stop them worrying, don't you think?

QUINCE: That's a good idea.

SNOUT: And the lion's another problem. The ladies will be very afraid of that, won't they?

STARVELING: I agree with you, Tom Snout.

BOTTOM: Yes, the lion's the most frightening animal in the world. We must do something about that to protect the ladies.

SNOUT: Before the play, you must tell them that it isn't a real lion.

BOTTOM: No, the audience must be able to see the actor's face through the lion's neck. He must speak to the ladies when he comes on the stage. He'll say, 'Ladies, don't be afraid. I'm not a real lion. I'm only Snug the bread-maker, dressed in a lion's skin.'

QUINCE: These things are easily done, but we have two more difficult problems. The first is this: Pyramus and Thisby must meet by moonlight. But how do we bring moonlight into the Duke's palace?

SNOUT: Will there be a full moon on the wedding night?

QUINCE: Yes, there will. I checked before we came.

BOTTOM: Good. If we open the palace windows, the moon can shine in onto the stage.

QUINCE: Or one of us can come in with a lantern in his hand. He can tell the audience that he's the moon. But there's a second problem. In the story, Pyramus and Thisby have to talk through a hole in the wall. So we have to bring a wall onto the stage.

SNOUT: You can't bring in a wall. What do you think, Bottom?

BOTTOM: One of us will have to be the wall. The actor can make a circle with his fingers and thumbs and Pyramus and Thisby can speak through that.

16

QUINCE: That's a good idea. Now, let's sit down and practise our lines. Pyramus, you begin. After your lines, go off stage and wait for Thisby to call you back. Now, is everybody ready?

[*Puck arrives. The actors don't see him.*]

PUCK: What's happening here, so near to the place where the Fairy Queen is sleeping? Oh, how exciting – it's a play! I'll watch it from here. Perhaps there'll be a part in it for me!

QUINCE: Speak, Pyramus. Thisby, get ready.

BOTTOM [*as Pyramus*]: The flowers of the forest taste so sweet.

QUINCE: *Smell* so sweet, not *taste*!

BOTTOM [*as Pyramus*]: The flowers of the forest smell so sweet, as sweet as the air from your mouth, dear Thisby. But listen, I can hear a voice. Wait here, Thisby, and I'll soon return. [*He leaves.*]

PUCK: That's the strangest Pyramus that I've ever seen! [*He leaves quietly.*]

FLUTE: Do I speak now?

QUINCE: Yes, you do. Pyramus will return after you speak.

FLUTE [*as Thisby*]: Oh, my wonderful snow-white, rose-red Pyramus, how can someone so young be so wise? I'll meet you, Pyramus, where dead Ninny lies . . .

QUINCE [*angrily*]: Where dead *Ninus* lies, not *Ninny*! And you mustn't say that line until Pyramus returns. [*shouting*] Pyramus, where are you? You're late!

[*Puck returns. He is followed by Bottom with a donkey's head on his shoulders.*]

BOTTOM [*as Pyramus*]: I am yours, fair Thisby. I will always belong to you.

QUINCE: Help! It's a monster! We must escape! Our lives are in danger!

[*All the actors run away.*]

PUCK [*laughing at the backs of the frightened actors*]: I'll follow you, and guide you in circles around this forest. Sometimes I'll be a horse, other times I'll be a dog, a headless lion, or a fire. I'll scream and roar. I'll burn everywhere you go! [*He leaves.*]

BOTTOM: Why have they all run away? Is this some kind of joke to make me afraid?

[*Snout comes back.*]

SNOUT: Oh, Bottom, you've changed! What do I see on your shoulders?

BOTTOM: What are you talking about? Do you think I'm a donkey?

[*Snout leaves. Quince comes back.*]

QUINCE: Oh, poor Bottom. What's happened to you? [*He leaves.*]

BOTTOM: I understand what they're trying to do. They're trying to make a donkey out of me. They're trying to frighten me, but I'm not afraid. I won't follow them. I'll walk up and down here, singing in a loud voice.

[*singing*] The female bird is small and brown,

The male is large and white.

One sings about a summer's day,

The other sings of night.

TITANIA [*waking up*]: What beautiful music has woken me from my sleep?

BOTTOM [*still singing*]: The baby bird is sitting

On a small stone by a lake.

It starts to sing but – oh, poor thing!

It's eaten by a snake!

TITANIA: Oh, please, don't stop singing! Your music is as beautiful to my ear as your face is to my eyes. I do believe, you handsome creature, that I'm in love with you.

BOTTOM: Madam, I don't know why you're saying that. When people fall in love, they seem to lose all their intelligence. But I

think that's a pity. Why can't love and intelligence go together?

TITANIA: You're as wise as you are beautiful.

BOTTOM: That's not true. If I'm wise, I'll be able to get out of this wood without any help.

TITANIA: Out of this wood? Oh no, please don't go. You must stay here with me. I'm not just an ordinary person – I'm a Fairy Queen. And I love you. If you stay with me, my fairies will look after you. They'll bring you gifts. They'll sing to you while you sleep on a bed of flowers. If you stay with me, you'll live for ever. Peaseblossom, Cobweb, Mustardseed, where are you?

[*Peaseblossom, Cobweb and Mustardseed arrive.*]

THE THREE FAIRIES: We're here.

TITANIA: Be kind and loving to this gentleman. Follow him when he takes a walk. Dance in front of his eyes. Feed him with the best fruit that you can find. Light fairy lanterns for him when he goes to bed. Guard him while he's sleeping. Keep the moonlight from his sleeping eyes. Give him everything that he needs. Greet him kindly.

THE THREE FAIRIES: Hello, fair stranger, and welcome.

BOTTOM: Thank you all very much. [*speaking to Cobweb*] And what's your name?

COBWEB: Cobweb.

BOTTOM: Young Mr Cobweb, you can be my doctor. If I cut my finger, I'll ask you for help. [*turning to Peaseblossom*] And who are you, my honest gentleman?

PEASEBLOSSOM: Peaseblossom.

BOTTOM: Young Mr Peaseblossom, greet your parents for me. [*turning to Mustardseed*] And what's your name, sir?

MUSTARDSEED: Mustardseed.

BOTTOM: Young Mr Mustardseed, I'm sure that we'll become good friends.

TITANIA [*to the three fairies*]: Come, look after him and bring him to my private garden. The moon looks sad tonight, I think. And when she cries, every little flower in the forest cries, too. They're sad because they have no love. So bring him to my garden quietly.

[*They all leave.*]

## Scene 2    *The place in the wood where Oberon and Titania met earlier*

[*Oberon arrives.*]

OBERON: I'm sure that Titania has woken up. What creature has she fallen in love with? [*Puck arrives.*] Here comes my messenger. What news have you got, my amusing little friend?

PUCK [*laughing*]: The Queen has fallen in love with a monster. While she was asleep in the wood, a group of Athenian workers arrived. They were practising a play for Theseus on his wedding night. When one of them went alone into the trees, I changed his head into a donkey's head for a joke. The others ran away when they saw him. But Titania wasn't afraid of him. When she woke up, she immediately fell in love with him!

OBERON [*laughing, too*]: That's excellent news! And the young Athenian man? Have you found him yet? Have you put the love-juice in his eyes?

PUCK: Yes, I found him easily. He was sleeping not far from the young woman.

[*Hermia and Demetrius arrive.*]

OBERON: Quickly, stand to one side. It's the Athenians.

PUCK [*interested*]: It's the same woman, but it's not the same man.

DEMETRIUS: Save your words for your enemies, not for me.

HERMIA: But I don't understand why Lysander disappeared so

suddenly. [*angrily*] What have you done with him? If you've killed him in his sleep, then kill me too!

DEMETRIUS: You think that I'm a murderer? No, the murderer is you. You're killing me with your cruel words. They cut into my heart more sharply than arrows.

HERMIA [*more softly*]: But where's Lysander? Oh, good Demetrius, where is he? Please give him back to me.

DEMETRIUS: I'd prefer to give his body to my dogs.

HERMIA [*angrily*]: So you *have* killed him! How did you do it? Did you kill him while he was sleeping? [*laughing coldly*] Oh, you brave man! All the snakes in the forest will be very proud of you.

DEMETRIUS [*feeling hurt*]: You're wrong to attack me like this. I'm not a murderer. Lysander's still alive.

HERMIA: Then tell me that he's well.

DEMETRIUS: And if I do, what will you promise me?

HERMIA: I promise that you'll never see me again. [*She leaves.*]

DEMETRIUS [*shaking his head, unable to understand*]: I can't follow her when she's feeling so angry with me. I'll rest here for a short time. All this suffering has made me tired and I need to sleep. [*He lies down and sleeps.*]

OBERON [*to Puck*]: What have you done? You've put love-juice in the wrong man's eyes! I wanted you to repair a broken love. But you've broken another love that was true!

PUCK [*smiling*]: Love's always like this. One man succeeds in keeping his promise but millions of others fail.

OBERON [*seriously*]: Go back into the wood faster than the wind. Find Helena of Athens and the poor man who is now in love with her. Bring them both here immediately.

PUCK: I'll travel faster than Cupid's arrow! [*He leaves.*]

OBERON [*putting the juice into Demetrius's eyes*]: Oh, purple flower of Cupid, fill this young man's heart with your special power. When he wakes, he'll see brave Helena. She'll seem to him as beautiful as the evening star.

[*Puck returns.*]

PUCK: My Lord, Helena is here with the young Athenian. Shall we watch them for a minute? Their conversation's very amusing.

OBERON: Stand to one side. [*listening*] They're making enough noise to wake Demetrius.

PUCK [*laughing*]: Then there will be two men in love with the same woman! This will be great fun!

[*Puck and Oberon hide behind a tree. Lysander and Helena arrive.*]

LYSANDER: Why do you think that I'm making fun of you? Look at my tears. Do they seem like a joke to you?

HELENA [*coldly*]: You're a good actor, Lysander, and you're very clever with words. But your promises of love belong to Hermia, not to me. How can you forget your love for her so quickly?

LYSANDER: I didn't really love her. I was crazy then. I didn't know real love until I saw you.

HELENA: Your words prove that you *still* don't know real love.

LYSANDER: Demetrius loves Hermia. He doesn't love you.

[*Demetrius wakes up.*]

DEMETRIUS: Oh Helena, my perfect dream, my beautiful princess! What can I compare you with? Snow seems black when I see the whiteness of your hand. The brightest summer's day seems dark and cloudy when I see the sunlight in your eyes. The reddest apple on the tree seems colourless and dry when I see the sweetness of your mouth.

I will die if I can't have this:

the softness of your loving kiss!

HELENA [*angrily*]: This is crazy! Do you both hate me so much? Why are you so cruel to me? How brave of you to bring so

*'Oh Helena, my perfect dream, my beautiful princess!'*

many tears to a young girl's eyes! I hope that you both feel proud of yourselves!

LYSANDER: Yes, stop being so unkind, Demetrius. I know that you've always loved Hermia. You can have her now – I won't stand in your way. But leave Helena for me, because I love her more than life itself.

HELENA: I've never heard a conversation as stupid as this!

DEMETRIUS: Lysander, you can keep your Hermia. My love for her has gone. My heart visited her like a travelling guest, but in Helena it has found its home.

LYSANDER: Helena, tell me that it isn't true!

DEMETRIUS: Don't laugh at a love too deep for you to understand. Look, here comes your love now. Go to her!

[*Hermia arrives.*]

HERMIA: The eye sees less in the darkness, but the ear hears so much more. Lysander, I heard your voice long before I saw your face. Why did you leave me alone in the wood so suddenly?

LYSANDER: How can a man stay when love tells him to go?

HERMIA: What love could take you from my side?

LYSANDER: My love for Helena. She brightens up the night more than a million stars. So why do you search for me, Hermia? Can't you see how much I hate you?

HERMIA [*very surprised*]: I don't believe I'm hearing this! You don't know what you're saying!

HELENA [*crying*]: I understand it all now. The three of you have planned this joke on me together. Hermia, how can you be so cruel? Have you forgotten everything? We were children together at school. I loved you like a sister. You've always been my dearest friend, but now you've joined my enemies in their sport! You're laughing at my unhappiness and enjoying every minute!

24

HERMIA: I'm not laughing at you, Helena. *You're* laughing at *me*!

HELENA: Who sent Lysander after me to fill my ears with untrue words of love? Why does Demetrius, your other love, suddenly call me a 'princess' and a 'perfect dream'? You told them to do these things to me, didn't you? But why? You know that I'm not as lucky as you. You have the love of two men and I have none. You should pity me, not laugh at me like this.

HERMIA: I don't know what you're talking about.

HELENA: Stop lying to me. I know what the three of you are really thinking. When I turn my back, you point your fingers at me. I'm not staying here. You can all laugh at me as loudly as you like. I'm leaving!

LYSANDER: Stay, Helena, and hear my excuse. My love, my life, my heart, my beautiful Helena!

HELENA [*coldly*]: Oh, excellent acting!

HERMIA: Lysander, stop making fun of her like this.

DEMETRIUS: Yes, if you don't stop this silly game, I'll stop it for you!

LYSANDER: What can *you* do to stop a love as great as this?

DEMETRIUS: No one loves Helena as much as I do!

LYSANDER: Then pull out your sword and prove it!

DEMETRIUS: I will!

HERMIA: Think, Lysander – where's all this going to end?

LYSANDER: Keep away from me, you stupid creature! If you come near me, I'll shake you from me like a snake!

DEMETRIUS: Don't be unkind. Haven't you already hurt her enough?

HERMIA: Oh, Lysander, what's happened to our sweet love?

LYSANDER: Sweet love? It was more like a bad-tasting medicine.

HERMIA: What cruel sport is this?

HELENA: The same cruel sport that you enjoy with me.

LYSANDER: Don't worry, Demetrius. I promise not to hurt Hermia.

DEMETRIUS: How can I believe the promises of a man who changes love so quickly?

LYSANDER: I'm not as dangerous as you think. I hate her – yes – but I'll never hurt her.

HERMIA: You loved me so much last night. Why do you suddenly hate me? I'm the same Hermia, but what's happened to my Lysander?

LYSANDER: Stop all these questions, and be sure of just one thing: I hate you, and I love Helena.

HERMIA [to Helena]: You thief of love! What have you done? Did you come last night and steal my lover's heart from him?

HELENA [angrily]: That's not true and you know it, you simple-minded little woman!

HERMIA: Little? Why do you call me 'little'? Oh, now I understand. You're taller, so you're better than me. Is that it? Lysander doesn't have to look down so far to see into your face. All right, it's true that I'm shorter than you. But I'm tall enough to push my fingers into your eyes!

HELENA [calmly]: Be sensible, good Hermia. Don't be so angry with me. I've always loved you like a sister. I've never done anything to hurt you – except, perhaps, for one thing. In my love for Demetrius, I told him about your plans to run away from Athens. He followed you into this wood, and I followed him. But I've suffered for my crime. Demetrius was angry with me and told me to leave him. I was afraid that he wanted to hit me. I want to go back to Athens now. It breaks my heart that my dear friends now all hate me.

HERMIA: Then go. What's stopping you?

HELENA: Only the love that I leave behind.

HERMIA: For Lysander?

HELENA: No, for Demetrius.

LYSANDER: Don't be afraid, Helena. Hermia won't hurt you.

HELENA: I'm not afraid. Hermia's always been like this. When we were at school, she often got angry very quickly. The other girls were frightened of her. She's small, but she's as brave as a lion.

HERMIA: 'Small' again! Always 'small' and 'little'! Come here, and I'll punish you for your rudeness!

LYSANDER [*rudely*]: Go away, you silly child, you little egg, you little ball of nothing!

DEMETRIUS: Why do you defend Helena? She doesn't love you, she doesn't need your help. If you continue to stand between Helena and me, you'll be sorry.

LYSANDER: Follow me into the wood, if you're brave enough. I'll prove with my sword that my love for Helena is stronger than yours!

DEMETRIUS: Follow you? No, I'll go with you side by side.

[*Demetrius and Lysander leave.*]

HERMIA [*angrily*]: They're going to fight because of you. You can't leave now.

HELENA: I don't feel safe alone in the forest with you. You'll attack me if I stay. But my legs are longer than yours and I can easily run away!

[*Helena leaves quickly, followed by Hermia. Oberon and Puck come out from behind the tree.*]

OBERON: This is all because of you. Was it an honest mistake, or did you put love-juice in the wrong man's eyes on purpose?

PUCK: It was an honest mistake, believe me. I followed your orders and put the love-juice in the eyes of a man from Athens. I didn't know that there were *two* Athenian men in the forest. But it's been good fun, hasn't it?

OBERON: Perhaps, but it's become too serious now. Those two men are going to have a sword fight and you must stop them. I want you to cover the moon with cloud and fill the forest with a thick, dark mist. Then call to each man in the other man's voice and guide them along different paths. When they're completely lost, they'll feel tired. They'll fall asleep. Put the juice of this flower into Lysander's eyes – it will take away the power of the other juice. When the two men wake up, everything will seem like a bad dream to them. They'll forget their stupid fight. Lysander will be in love with Hermia again and Demetrius will still be in love with Helena. And I'll find Titania and ask her for the Indian boy. Then I'll put this juice in her eyes, too. She'll stop loving that ugly creature and everybody will be happy again.

PUCK: My Fairy Lord, I'll do everything that you ask.

OBERON: But be quick because it's almost morning. We must finish our work before the sun comes up. [*He leaves.*]

PUCK: Up and down, up and down,
    I will take them up and down.
    In a mist their fight will end,
    Enemies will soon be friends.
    But look – here comes the first one.

[*Puck leaves. Lysander arrives.*]

LYSANDER: Where are you, proud Demetrius?

PUCK [*in Demetrius's voice from off-stage*]: I'm over here. Get your sword ready and prepare to defend yourself!

LYSANDER: I'm ready for you!

PUCK [*as Demetrius*]: Follow me – there's a better place for fighting over here.

[*Lysander leaves. Demetrius arrives.*]

DEMETRIUS: Lysander, speak again. Show me where you are. Or are you running away from me? Are you too afraid to fight?

PUCK [*in Lysander's voice from off-stage*]: No, *you're* the frightened one! You shout brave words at the shadows. But you're not brave enough to shout them at me!

DEMETRIUS: Where are you?

PUCK [*as Lysander*]: Follow my voice. I know a better place than this for a war.

[*Demetrius leaves. Lysander returns.*]

LYSANDER: This is impossible. I've followed Demetrius's voice, but I still can't find him. He's too fast for me and now I'm completely lost. I think I'll rest here. I'll look for him in the morning.

[*Lysander lies down and sleeps. Puck returns and hides behind a tree. Demetrius returns.*]

PUCK [*in Lysander's voice*]: Ho, ho, ho, you frightened little creature! Why don't you come and find me?

DEMETRIUS [*unable to see Puck or Lysander*]: I'll find you if you stop running away from me. Where are you now?

PUCK [*as Lysander*]: I'm over here.

DEMETRIUS: Oh, I'm too tired for more of this. I'm going to rest here. But be careful – I'll find you in the morning and then you'll be sorry!

[*Demetrius lies down and sleeps. Helena returns.*]

HELENA: Oh, long and boring night, when will daylight come? I want to get out of this ugly wood and away from the terrible people inside it. Perhaps if I sleep here, I can forget my sadness until morning. [*She lies down and sleeps.*]

PUCK: I have three unhappy lovers, but I want one more.
    I can't do anything until there are four. [*Hermia arrives.*]
    Ah, here comes the picture of unhappiness.
    Cupid is cruel, but his jokes are the best!

HERMIA: I'm so tired that I can't continue. I've looked everywhere for Lysander but I can't find him. I'll have to rest here until the morning. I hope that Lysander stays safely away from Demetrius's sword. [*She lies down and sleeps.*]

PUCK [*going down on his knees next to Lysander*]: While you're sleeping, I'll put this flower-juice in your eyes. When you open them in the morning, you'll be in love with Hermia again. Tonight will seem like a strange dream to you all, and the world will be a very happy place! [*He leaves.*]

## Act 4  Bottom's Dream

### Scene 1  *The same part of the wood*

[*Demetrius, Lysander, Helen and Hermia are still asleep. Titania and her fairies arrive with Bottom. Bottom still has his donkey's head.*]

TITANIA: Come and sit next to me on this bed of flowers. I want to touch your handsome face and kiss your lovely big ears.

BOTTOM: Where's Peaseblossom?

PEASEBLOSSOM: I'm ready.

BOTTOM: I'm tired. Touch my aching head with your pretty little fingers. Cobweb?

COBWEB: I'm ready.

BOTTOM: I'm thirsty. Bring me a small cup of raindrops from the prettiest flowers in the wood. Mustardseed?

MUSTARDSEED: I'm ready.

BOTTOM: My face feels very hairy tonight. Shave me with your little silver knife.

TITANIA: Wait. Would you like to hear some music, my sweet love?

BOTTOM: Yes, I love good music. Play me some songs.

[*Romantic music plays.*]

TITANIA: Now, my love, what would you like to eat?

'I want to touch your handsome face and kiss your lovely big ears.'

BOTTOM: Dry grass – lots of it!

TITANIA: I have a brave fairy who will look for something better for you. Fresh fruit, perhaps? Or would you like her to steal some cake for you from the village?

BOTTOM: No, I'd prefer grass. But don't worry about it now. I have an urgent need for sleep.

TITANIA: Sleep, then, and I'll hold you in my arms. Fairies, leave us now. [*The fairies leave.*] Oh, I love you so much! I'll do anything for you!

[*The music stops. Titania sleeps with Bottom in her arms. Oberon and Puck arrive.*]

OBERON: This is very amusing – my Queen with a donkey in her arms! But I'm beginning to pity her now. A short time ago, I met them both in the wood. I made fun of her for putting flowers all over his hairy face. But she didn't get angry. She smiled at me sweetly, her heart filled with for this ugly creature. I asked her then for the Indian boy, and she agreed immediately. She sent one of her fairies to take him to my home. I have the boy, so now I'll take away the power of the love-juice from her eyes. Then, my good friend Puck, you'll take the donkey's head away from this man's shoulders. He'll wake up, go back to Athens with the others and forget about this strange night. But first I must free the Fairy Queen from her strange dreams. [*He goes down on his knees next to Titania.*]

Be what you want to be.

See what you want to see.

With this juice I take the power

Of Cupid's dangerous purple flower.

Now Titania, my sweet Queen, wake up.

TITANIA [*waking up*]: Oberon, I've had a really strange dream. I dreamt that I was in love with a donkey!

OBERON: It wasn't a dream. Look, your love is sleeping next to you.

TITANIA: Oh, how did this terrible thing happen? How could I love an ugly creature like this?

OBERON: Puck, take off the creature's head. Titania, call for some music.

[*Music plays.*]

PUCK [*on his knees next to Bottom*]: Now, when you wake up, you'll be a simple-minded cloth-maker again.

OBERON: What lovely music! Come, my Queen, take my hand and dance with me. Now you and I are friends again, we'll dance together at Theseus's wedding tomorrow night. The two pairs of lovers will also be there, and we'll all dance to the music of love!

PUCK: Listen, Fairy King, I can hear the first bird of the morning.

OBERON: So, my Queen, in sad silence we must leave this wood behind us. We'll follow the night around the world, flying faster than the moon.

TITANIA: Come, my Lord. As we fly,
    Answer this. Do not lie!
    How did a man with a donkey's head
    Find his way into my bed?

[*Oberon, Titania and Puck leave. The sleepers lie without moving. Theseus, Egeus and Hippolyta arrive with Theseus's courtiers.*]

THESEUS [*to his courtiers*]: One of you go and find the forester. I want my future wife to hear the wonderful sound of my dogs running after wild animals in the forest. [*to Hippolyta*] Fair Queen, you and I will go up to the mountain top. We will have a better view of the animals from there. But wait – who are these people sleeping here?

EGEUS: My Lord, this is my daughter. The two men are Lysander and Demetrius. And this is Helena, old Nedar's daughter. I am surprised to see them all together like this.

THESEUS: Perhaps they got up early to enjoy the first morning in May. But Egeus, today is the day when Hermia must decide between marriage to Demetrius and death. Am I right?

EGEUS: You are, my good Lord.

THESEUS [*turning to his courtiers*]: Wake them up. [*Four courtiers wake the sleepers up.*] Good morning, friends. What is this? Is it now the time for young lovers?

LYSANDER [*sleepily*]: Forgive us, my Lord.

THESEUS: Please stand up, all of you. [*to Lysander and Demetrius*] I know that you two are enemies. Why are you happy to sleep so close together?

LYSANDER: My Lord, I'm as surprised as you are. But if I can remember correctly, I came here with Hermia last night. We planned to escape from Athens and its dangerous laws.

EGEUS: I have heard enough, my Lord. Did you hear what this young man just said? He wanted to escape the law of Athens! He wanted to steal my daughter from me! You must punish him, and my daughter, too!

DEMETRIUS: My Lord, fair Helena told me about their plans. I was angry and followed them into this wood. But something strange has happened, my Lord, and I cannot explain it. My love for Hermia seems to me like an old memory. Now, my heart is filled with love for Helena. I promised to marry her before I met Hermia. Then, suddenly, I thought that I was in love with Hermia. I left Helena, and asked Hermia to marry me. But I was crazy, like a sick man who has lost interest in his food. This morning, I have returned to health. I realize that I have never stopped loving Helena.

[*Helena looks at Demetrius with surprise. Then she smiles and takes his hand.*]

THESEUS [*happily*]: So, Egeus, it seems that it is not necessary to punish anyone. Demetrius is happy with Helena, and Lysander with Hermia. Tonight, these happy lovers will join Hippolyta and me in the palace. Three husbands will marry three wives. Let's forget about looking for wild animals today. We shall return to Athens and all six of us will eat together before our wedding night!

[*Theseus, Hippolyta, Egeus and the assistants leave.*]

DEMETRIUS [*shaking his head slowly with surprise*]: Everything this morning seems very strange. Things look ordinary, but there's something different about them, too. Don't you agree?

HERMIA [*smiling nervously as Lysander shyly takes her hand*]: Yes, I do. Something mysterious has happened to us. There are so many unanswered questions.

HELENA [*holding Demetrius's hand*]: I agree. Demetrius loves me, but I don't know how. He's mine at last, but in many ways he isn't. What's happened to us?

DEMETRIUS: Are you sure that we're awake? Perhaps we're still asleep and dreaming? Was Theseus really here? Did he really invite us to follow him?

HERMIA: Yes, and my father, too.

HELENA: And Hippolyta.

LYSANDER: He told us to follow him to the palace.

DEMETRIUS [*happily*]: Then we *are* awake! Come, let's follow him. And on the way we can all discuss our dreams.

[*They leave. Bottom wakes up.*]

BOTTOM: When you want Pyramus on the stage, call me. I'll be ready. I'm waiting for Thisby to say, 'Fairest Pyramus . . .' But wait a minute. Where is everybody? Peter Quince? Flute the shoe-mender? Snout the tool-mender? Starveling? They've all run away and left me here alone. How selfish of them! Why didn't they wake me up first? Ah, but I've just had the strangest dream. How can I explain it? If I try, I'll seem as stupid as a donkey. I thought that I was ... what? Who can say? I thought that I had ... what? People will laugh if I try to explain. Man's eye hasn't heard, his ear hasn't seen, his hand can't taste and his tongue can't understand the meaning of my dream. I'll tell Peter Quince to write a song about it. I'll call it 'Bottom's Dream' – because it has no bottom. I'll sing it for the Duke and the Duchess during the play. Or perhaps it will be better if I sing it at the end ... [*He leaves.*]

## Scene 2    *The market square in Athens*

[*Quince, Flute, Snout and Starveling arrive.*]

QUINCE: Has Bottom returned yet?
STARVELING: No one's seen him.
FLUTE: If he doesn't come back, how can we do our play?
QUINCE: We can't. No one in Athens can play Pyramus better than Bottom can.
FLUTE: I agree. He's the funniest and cleverest man in the city.
QUINCE: Yes, and the best singer, too.

[*Snug arrives.*]

SNUG: The Duke and the Duchess have just got married. Two other pairs of lovers got married at the same time. All six of them are at the palace, having dinner. They'll soon be ready for us – but why isn't Bottom here? We can't do our play without him!
QUINCE: I know. He's a silly man. The Duke's paying us well to do this play. But no one will get a penny if Bottom isn't here.

[*Bottom arrives.*]

BOTTOM: What's the matter? Why do you all look so worried?
QUINCE: Bottom! Oh, wonderful day! Happy hour!

BOTTOM: Gentlemen, I've had a really strange adventure. But don't ask me to talk about it. You'll think that I'm crazy.

QUINCE: Tell us, Bottom. What happened?

BOTTOM: Not now – we haven't much time. The Duke has finished eating and we must get ready for the palace. I hope we've all learnt our lines. Hurry up and get all your things. And, dearest actors, please don't eat anything smelly before we go on stage. The air from our mouths must smell sweet as we say our words. Then the audience will say, 'This is the sweetest play we've ever seen!' Now, no more words. Let's go, and I'll meet you all at the palace.

## Act 5   Pyramus and Thisby

### Scene 1   *A large room in Theseus's palace*

[*Theseus, Hippolyta, Philostrate and some Lords arrive.*]

HIPPOLYTA: Those lovers speak of mysterious things, don't they, Theseus?

THESEUS: Strange things, yes, but none of it is true. Lovers, crazy people and the writers of poems believe in these silly fairy stories, but I don't. They can imagine things that reason will never understand. The crazy man sees monsters that have never existed. The lover believes that the ugliest creature in the forest is beautiful. The writer of poems looks at the sky and imagines impossible things. He pours these dreams into his pen and gives them a shape and a name. But these things are not real. The mind can play strange games with you when you are afraid in the middle of the night. In the darkness, you can easily believe that a tree is a terrible monster.

HIPPOLYTA: But the lovers all repeat the same story. If everybody believes the same thing, it suddenly becomes real. It does not matter how unbelievable it seems.

[*Lysander, Demetrius, Hermia and Helena arrive.*]

THESEUS: Here come the lovers, laughing happily. Welcome, my good friends.

LYSANDER: Thank you, my Lord.

THESEUS: Come now, we have three long hours to fill between dinner and bedtime. What games and dancing shall we have? [*turning to Philostrate*] Philostrate?

PHILOSTRATE: Yes, my Lord.

THESEUS: Tell me, what pleasant things have you planned for this evening? Is there any music? Are there any plays?

PHILOSTRATE: I have planned a few things for you. You can choose which one you want to see first.

LYSANDER: A young Athenian man will sing a song in a very high voice. It's about a fight with monsters – half-horses, half-men.

THESEUS: No, I do not want that. My wife already knows that song. I have sung it to her many times.

LYSANDER: Would you prefer the wild dance of the Romans? They drink too much wine and attack a Greek singer.

THESEUS [*looking bored*]: That is an old dance. I have seen it many times before.

LYSANDER: There are the three princesses. They make a sad speech about the death of Learning.

THESEUS: No, that is too sad for a wedding night.

LYSANDER: There is a short, boring play about young Pyramus and his love for Thisby. It is a sad story, but funny in all the wrong places.

THESEUS: Funny but sad? Boring but short? This seems interesting! Tell me about it.

PHILOSTRATE: The play is about ten words long, my Lord, but

that is ten words too many. The words have no meaning and the actors are terrible. There is a sad bit in the story when Pyramus kills himself. I saw them practising the scene and my eyes were filled with tears. But I was not crying because it was sad. I was crying because it was so funny!

THESEUS: Who are the actors?

PHILOSTRATE: They are all men who work in the market. They are not very clever. It is difficult for them to remember their lines.

THESEUS: Then let us hear it.

PHILOSTRATE: No, my Lord, it is not for you. I have seen it, and it is completely useless. You will only laugh at it.

THESEUS: I want to see the play. These simple-minded men have worked hard for their Duke's wedding. Bring them in, and take your seats, my Ladies.

[*Philostrate leaves. Helena, Hermia and Hippolyta sit down facing the stage. Demetrius, Lysander and Theseus sit down next to them. Egeus and other Lords sit down behind them.*]

HIPPOLYTA: I do not enjoy making fun of poor people. When they try something too difficult, they look stupid.

THESEUS: Sweet Hippolyta, they will not look stupid.

HIPPOLYTA: But Philostrate says that the play is useless.

THESEUS: Then it is even more important for us to thank them. It does not matter how good the play is. We must thank them for trying. In my life, I have met many people who have prepared great speeches of welcome for me. But when they see me, they become nervous. Their bodies shake, their faces go pale and they say nothing. But I still find words of welcome in their silence. In the same way, I can hear great art in the simple language of unintelligent people. So let us enjoy the play.

[*Philostrate returns.*]

PHILOSTRATE: My Lord, are you ready for the play to begin?
THESEUS: Yes. Let us see the first actor.

[*There is the sound of music. Quince steps onto the stage in front of Theseus and his guests.*]

QUINCE [*talking very quickly*]: If our play makes you angry, we're sorry. We want you to be amused, not angry. We want to show you our simple skill. This is our plan. We want you to enjoy our play. That's why we're here. The actors are ready. From our little play, you'll learn many things. You won't be sorry that you've seen our play. We hope that you won't be angry.

THESEUS [*quietly to Lysander*]: He speaks very quickly, doesn't he?

LYSANDER: He's ridden his lines like a wild, young horse. He doesn't know when to stop.

HIPPOLYTA: He is like a child playing music – a lot of noise, but no meaning.

THESEUS: The words are correct, but they are in the wrong order. [*to Quince*] Who is next?

[*The actors arrive on the stage: Bottom, dressed as Pyramus, is carrying a sword. Flute, as Thisby, is dressed like a woman. Snout, as the wall, has a big picture of a wall hanging round his neck. Starveling, as the moon, is carrying a lantern and has a dog with him. Snug is dressed as a lion. You can see his face through the lion's neck.*]

QUINCE: Perhaps you don't know who these people are. Don't worry – I'll introduce them. [*pointing to Bottom*] This man is Pyramus. [*Bottom steps towards the audience, waves his sword and smiles. Quince points to Flute.*] This beautiful lady is Thisby. [*Flute steps towards the audience and smiles. Quince points to Snout.*] This man is the wall that stands cruelly between the two lovers. [*Snout holds out his hand and makes a circle with his finger and thumb.*] The unhappy lovers have to talk through this hole in the wall. [*pointing to Starveling*] This man with the lantern and the dog is the moon. [*Starveling waves his lantern at the audience.*] The young lovers often meet by moonlight in the place where dead Ninus lies. [*pointing to Snug*] This frightening creature is the lion who frightens lovely Thisby with his roar. [*Snug jumps towards the audience and roars.*] As she runs away, she drops her coat. The lion takes it in his mouth and covers it in blood from his teeth. Pyramus finds the blood-covered coat. He thinks that his lover is dead. He takes his sword and kills himself. Thisby watches this from her hiding-place in the trees. She takes her lover's sword and kills herself. Now we're ready to act this very sad story.

[*All the actors leave except Snout.*]

THESEUS [*to Demetrius*]: Do you think that the lion is going to speak?

DEMETRIUS: If donkeys can, why not a lion?

SNOUT [*as the wall*]: My name is Snout and I'm the wall. [*showing the audience his finger and thumb*] And this is the hole that Pyramus and Thisby secretly speak through.

THESEUS [*smiling to Demetrius*]: Have you ever heard a wall speak better than this?

DEMETRIUS: It's the cleverest wall that I've ever seen.

[*Bottom, as Pyramus, comes in.*]

THESEUS: Pyramus is moving towards the wall. Listen.

BOTTOM [*as Pyramus*]: Oh, dark, black night. Oh, night, you are always here when day is not. Oh, night, I am afraid that Thisby has forgotten her promise. And you, wall, oh, sweet and lovely wall, you stand between her father's ground and mine. Oh, sweet and lovely wall, show me your little hole. I want to look through it with my eye. [*looking through the 'hole in the wall'*] Thank you, kind wall. But what do I see? Thisby is not here! Oh, terrible wall, I see no happiness through you! I hate you!

THESEUS [*to Bottom*]: The wall must answer you.

BOTTOM [*stepping away from the wall*]: No, sir, he mustn't. Thisby's going to come in now and I'm going to see her through the wall. Look, here she comes.

[*Flute, as Thisby, comes in.*]

FLUTE [*as Thisby, in a very high voice*]: Oh, wall, you have often heard my sad words because you stand between fair Pyramus and me. My rose-red mouth has often kissed your stone.

BOTTOM [*as Pyramus*]: I can see a voice. I will go to the hole in the wall to hear my Thisby's face. [*looking through the hole*] Thisby?

FLUTE [*as Thisby*]: My love, you are my love, I think.

BOTTOM [*as Pyramus*]: I am your love. [*putting his mouth to the hole in the wall*] Oh, kiss me through the hole of this cruel wall.

FLUTE [*as Thisby, putting his mouth to the hole in the wall*]: I am kissing the wall's hole, not your mouth.

BOTTOM [*as Pyramus*]: Will you meet me where dead Ninny lies?

FLUTE [*as Thisby*]: I will go there immediately.

[*Bottom and Flute leave.*]

SNOUT [*as the wall*]: That is the end of the wall's part in this play. So, with these words, the wall will go away. [*He leaves.*]

HIPPOLYTA: This is the silliest play that I have ever seen.

THESEUS: With a little imagination, it seems very good.

HIPPOLYTA: Yes, but we must use *our* imagination, not theirs.

THESEUS: Think of them as they think of themselves. Then we can imagine that they are excellent men. Look – the moon and the lion are coming.

[*Snug, as the lion, and Starveling, as the moon, come in.*]

SNUG [*as the lion*]: Ladies, you'll probably feel frightened when you see me. You'll shake with fear when you hear my roar. But don't be afraid because the lion's really me, Snug the bread-maker.

'Oh, kiss me through the hole of this cruel wall.'

THESEUS [to Demetrius and Lysander]: A very kind lion.

DEMETRIUS: The politest lion that I've ever seen.

LYSANDER: But he doesn't seem very brave.

THESEUS: True. And his honesty destroys the excitement of the story. But listen – the moon is going to speak.

STARVELING [as the moon]: This lantern's the moon, not me. I'm just a man.

THESEUS [to Demetrius and Lysander]: Ah, this is the greatest mistake of all. The man must climb inside the lantern. Then he will be the Man in the Moon!

DEMETRIUS: He's afraid to go too near the light. It doesn't look very strong.

HIPPOLYTA: I am tired of this moon. Can we have a different one?

THESEUS: It seems, from the weak light inside the lantern, that the moon is going to disappear. But we must be polite. We must imagine that it is shining brightly.

LYSANDER [to Starveling]: Continue your speech, moon.

STARVELING [as the moon]: I only want to tell you that this lantern's the moon. I'm the Man in the Moon. And this dog belongs to me.

[Flute, as Thisby, comes in.]

FLUTE [as Thisby]: This is the place where dead Ninny lies. Where is my love?

SNUG [as the lion, forgetting his lines]: Oh.

FLUTE [quietly to Snug]: You have to roar!

[Snug, as the lion, roars. Flute, as Thisby, screams. Then he runs away, leaving his coat on the ground.]

DEMETRIUS: Well roared, lion!

THESEUS: A wonderful escape, Thisby!

HIPPOLYTA: Well shone, moon! I have changed my mind about him. He shines beautifully!

44

[*Snug, as the lion, bites Thisby's coat and shakes it in his mouth. Then he leaves.*]

THESEUS: Well bitten, lion!

DEMETRIUS: Here comes Pyramus.

LYSANDER: That's why the lion has run away.

[*Bottom, as Pyramus, comes in.*]

BOTTOM [*as Pyramus*]: Sweet moon, thank you for your sunny light. In your shining, golden light, I hope to see fair Thisby. But wait, what is this terrible thing that I see on the ground at my feet? No! It cannot be! My dearest Thisby's coat is covered in blood! Oh, this is the end! My life is broken and destroyed!

THESEUS [*to Hippolyta*]: These strong feelings, and the death of a dear friend . . . He almost looks sad.

HIPPOLYTA: This is bad for my heart. I feel sorry for the man.

BOTTOM [*as Pyramus, waving his arms and crying with unhappiness*]: Oh, lions are terrible creatures! Why do they exist? A cold-hearted lion has eaten the love of my life! She is – no, she *was* – the fairest lady that ever lived! Come, tears, fill my eyes! Come, sword, push your sharp point deep into my chest – yes, the left side of my chest – and cut me to my heart! [*pushing the sword into his chest many times*] Again! Again! Again! And so I die, and now I am dead, and my heart has flown into the sky. Stop talking, tongue. Run away, moon. [*Starveling, as the moon, leaves.*] Now die, die, die, die, die. [*He falls to the floor.*]

LYSANDER: He's dead. He's nothing.

THESEUS: With the help of a doctor, he will get better. Then he will see what a donkey he has been!

HIPPOLYTA: The moon has gone. How will Thisby be able to find her lover?

[*Flute, as Thisby, comes in.*]

THESEUS: She will find him by the light of the stars. Look – here she comes. Her speech is the last one in the play.

HIPPOLYTA: I hope it is a short one.

LYSANDER: She's seen him already with those sweet eyes of hers.

FLUTE [*as Thisby, speaking softly*]: Asleep, my love? [*suddenly worried*] Or are you dead? [*going down on his knees and shaking Pyramus*] Oh, Pyramus, get up! Speak to me, speak to me! Oh no, he does not say a word. [*standing slowly*] Death has covered his eyes. His flower-soft mouth, his rose-red nose, his milk-white skin, are gone, are gone! Lovers, you must start to cry. Tongue, be silent. [*taking Pyramus's sword*] Come, sharp sword, and push your point into my breaking heart. [*He pushes the sword into his chest.*] And so, dear friends, this is Thisby's end. Goodbye, goodbye, goodbye.

THESEUS: The moon and the lion will have to put the dead lovers into the ground.

DEMETRIUS: The wall can help them, too.

BOTTOM [*from the floor*]: No, the wall has fallen down. Now, would you like to hear the final speech, or watch a special dance?

THESEUS: No final speech, thank you – there is nothing to explain. The lovers are dead, and there is no need for more discussion. Perhaps next time, Pyramus can tie one of Thisby's socks around his neck and kill himself with that. *That* will make the story even sadder. But your play is already excellent, gentlemen. Now, I am impatient to see your special dance. [*Starveling with his lantern and Snout with the picture of the wall around his neck dance for the Duke and the Duchess. It is a sad, slow dance that seems to last for ever. After a minute, Theseus stands up and the music stops.*] It is midnight, time for lovers to go to bed and for fairies to play in the moonlight. The play has amused us well this evening, but we have two more weeks of music, food and dancing every night. And so, sweet friends, goodnight.

[*Everybody leaves. Puck comes in.*]

PUCK [*to the audience*]: Now the hungry lion roars,
    The dog looks at the moon.
    The tired farmer is asleep –
    His heavy work is done.
    Now it is the time of night
    For hidden, secret sounds.
    Nervous people lock their doors
    And dead men leave the ground.
    Fairies love this time of night.
    They play and have great fun.
    They're following the darkness
    And running from the sun.
    And I am sent to watch this door
    And sweep the shadows from the floor.

[*Oberon, Titania and their fairies come in.*]

OBERON: Fill the house with lantern-light.
    Fairies, leave the trees.
    Come into the palace
    And sing and dance with me.
TITANIA: Fill the air with music.
    Fill the house with light.
    Fill the sleepy lovers' heads
    With happy dreams tonight.
OBERON: Now, until the sun comes up,
    We shall dance and sing.
    The lovers will not see us
    But they'll remember everything.
    Take this special love-juice
    To every man and wife.
    It will bring them good luck

And a long and happy life.
So, fairies, do your business.
When our work is done,
We'll fly away together
Before we see the sun.

[*All the fairies leave except Puck.*]

PUCK [*to the audience*]: Perhaps you have not understood
The things that you have seen.
Close your eyes, imagine
Everything is just a dream.
The darkness isn't frightening,
The shadows are not deep.
You mustn't be afraid
If you can see us in your sleep.
Are you angry with our story?
Do you think it isn't true?
As I am an honest Puck,
I have these words for you:
Forgive me, offer me your hands –
I want to be your friend.
And goodnight, everybody –
Our story's reached its end.

# ACTIVITIES

## Act 1

*Before you read*

1 *A Midsummer Night's Dream* is one of Shakespeare's most famous plays. What other Shakespeare plays do you know? What are they about? Are they amusing or sad?

2 Look at the Word List at the back of the book. Which are words for:

 a people?

 b dangerous animals?

 c the world of theatre?

 d things that you fight with?

 e things that do not exist?

3 Read the Introduction to the play. Which words on the right complete each sentence?

| | |
|---|---|
| a Theseus is | a fairy. |
| b Hermia does not want to marry | an actor. |
| c Hermia runs away with | a duke. |
| d Oberon and Titania are | midsummer. |
| e Shakespeare was | Demetrius. |
| f May 1st was | a great writer. |
| g Puck is | Lysander. |
| h Bottom is | fairies. |

*While you read*

4 Who are these sentences about?

 a They are going to be married.                      ........................

 b He tells the Duke about a problem.               ........................

 c Hermia loves him.                                        ........................

 d Demetrius wants to marry her.                      ........................

 e Helena loves him.                                        ........................

 f Lysander loves her.                                      ........................

 g They plan to run away.                                 ........................

 h He is going to play the part of Pyramus.       ........................

 i He is going to play the part of Thisby.           ........................

49

*After you read*

5 Use the best question-word for these questions, and then answer them.

What      Where      Who      Why

   a ......... sang at a window by moonlight?
   b ......... is Lysander's opinion of Demetrius?
   c ......... does Theseus want to talk to Demetrius?
   d ......... does Lysander's aunt live?
   e ......... do Lysander and Hermia want to run away?
   f ......... is Helena's plan?
   g ......... do the workers meet in the market square?
   h ......... are the workers going to practise their play?

6 Work with another student. Have this conversation.

   *Student A:*   You are Egeus. You think that power and money are more important than love in a marriage. Tell your daughter why.

   *Student B:*   You are Hermia. You think that love is more important than power and money in a marriage. Tell your father why.

7 Discuss these questions with another student. What do you think?

   a Is it right for a father to choose a husband for his daughter? Why (not)?
   b Is Hermia right to tell Helena her secret plan? Why (not)?
   c Who do you feel most sorry for? Why?

## Act 2

*Before you read*

8 What problems do you think Lysander and Hermia will have in the palace wood? Why?

*While you read*

**9** Number these in the correct order, 1–8.

   **a** Lysander and Hermia fall asleep in the wood. .....

   **b** Puck gives Oberon a special flower. .....

   **c** Demetrius is rude to Helena. .....

   **d** Puck puts love-juice in Lysander's eyes. .....

   **e** Titania and Oberon have a fight in the wood. .....

   **f** Oberon puts love-juice in Titania's eyes. .....

   **g** Lysander falls in love with Helena. .....

   **h** Oberon decides to help Helena. .....

*After you read*

**10** Are these sentences right or wrong? Correct the ones that are wrong.

   **a** Oberon is angry with Titania for stealing one of his courtiers.

   **b** Oberon's fight with Titania has changed the weather.

   **c** Cupid's arrow changed the colour of a flower.

   **d** Oberon wants Titania to fall in love with him.

   **e** Helena thinks that Demetrius is cruel.

   **f** Oberon thinks that Helena's problem is amusing.

   **g** Puck solves Helena's problem.

   **h** Helena believes that Lysander is in love with her.

**11** At the end of Act 2, are these people happy or unhappy? Why?

Hermia   Helena   Lysander   Demetrius   Oberon   Puck   Egeus

**12** In the fight between Oberon and Titania, who do you think is right? Why?

## Act 3

*Before you read*

**13** Discuss these questions with another student. What problems will there be for:

   **a** Puck, when he meets Oberon?

   **b** Titania, when she wakes up?

   **c** Hermia, when she meets Lysander?

   **d** Helena, when she meets Hermia?

   **e** the actors, when they practise in the wood?

**14** Work with another student. Have this conversation.

    *Student A:*   You are Hermia. What do you say to Lysander when you find him?

    *Student B:*   You are Lysander. What do you say to Hermia when she finds you?

*While you read*

**15** Who is speaking? Who or what are they talking about?

  **a** 'We must do something about that to protect the ladies.'

      ......................... is talking about ................................................

  **b** 'What do I see on your shoulders?'

      ......................... is talking about ................................................

  **c** 'Light fairy-lanterns for him when he goes to bed.'

      ......................... is talking about ................................................

  **d** 'When she cries, every little flower in the forest cries, too.'

      ......................... is talking about ................................................

  **e** 'If you've killed him in his sleep, then kill me, too!'

      ......................... is talking about ................................................

  **f** 'This will be great fun!'

      ......................... is talking about ................................................

  **g** 'Do you both hate me so much?'

      ......................... is talking about ................................................

  **h** 'My love for her has gone.'

      ......................... is talking about ................................................

  **i** 'Guide them along different paths.'

      ......................... is talking about ................................................

  **j** 'Here comes the picture of unhappiness.'

      ......................... is talking about ................................................

*After you read*

**16** Choose the correct answer.

  **a** In the play, Bottom is
- a donkey.
- a lion.
- a man.

  **b** When the actors run away, Bottom feels
- afraid.
- brave.
- worried.

  **c** Titania wakes up because she
- has a strange dream.
- hears a strange song.
- feels a snake on her skin.

  **d** Puck put love-juice in Lysander's eyes because
- he wanted to make trouble.
- he found the wrong man.
- Oberon told him to.

  **e** Demetrius says nice things to Helena because
- he feels sorry for her.
- he wants to protect her.
- Oberon has put love-juice in his eyes.

**17** Use these words in the sentences below.

afraid  amusing  angry  beautiful  clever  cruel  pleased
sad  serious  unkind  wise

  **a** The audience will feel ......... when they see the lion.
  **b** Quince thinks that Bottom's ideas are ......... .
  **c** Titania thinks that Bottom is ......... and ......... .
  **d** Titania thinks that the moon looks ......... .
  **e** Oberon is ......... when he hears about Titania.
  **f** Demetrius cannot understand why Hermia is ......... with him.
  **g** Puck thinks that the lovers' problems are ......... .
  **h** Helena thinks that Lysander and Demetrius are ......... .
  **i** Demetrius tells Lysander not to be ......... to Hermia.
  **j** Oberon thinks that the lovers' problems have become ......... .

**Act 4**

**18** Discuss these questions with another student. What do you think?

    **a** Will the flower-juice in Lysander's eyes solve all the lovers' problems?

    **b** What will happen with Titania and Bottom?

**19** Who do you think will say these words? Who to?

    **a** 'I want to ... kiss your lovely big ears.'

    **b** 'I asked her then for the Indian boy, and she agreed.'

    **c** 'You must punish him, and my daughter, too!'

    **d** 'Now, my heart is filled with love for Helena.'

*While you read*

**20** Circle the correct word.

    **a** Bottom wants to eat *grass / fruit*.

    **b** Bottom feels very *hungry / tired*.

    **c** Titania is *pleased / unhappy* that she loved Bottom.

    **d** *Oberon / Puck* takes off Bottom's head.

    **e** Helena is *amused / surprised* that Demetrius loves her.

    **f** The four lovers *remember / don't remember* their adventures.

    **g** Bottom wants to *write / sing* a song for the Duke's wedding.

    **h** Bottom *tells / doesn't tell* the others about his adventure.

*After you read*

**21** What problems did these people have together? How were they solved?

    **a** Oberon and Titania

    **b** Lysander and Hermia

    **c** Demetrius and Helena

    **d** Egeus and Hermia

**22** Work with another student. Have this conversation.

    *Student A:* You are Bottom. Explain to Quince why you are late for the play.

    *Student B:* You are Quince. You think that Bottom's story is crazy. Tell him why.

**Act 5**

**23** Will Theseus enjoy *Pyramus and Thisby*? Why (not)?

*While you read*

**24** Are these sentences right (✓) or wrong (✗)?

   **a** Theseus and Hippolyta have heard the lovers' story.    .....

   **b** Three princesses make a sad speech.    .....

   **c** Philostrate thinks that *Pyramus and Thisby* is amusing.    .....

   **d** Quince speaks his lines well.    .....

   **e** Starveling has a picture of the moon around his neck.    .....

   **f** Theseus thinks that the lion is not frightening enough.    .....

   **g** In the play, Thisby is killed by the lion.    .....

   **h** The fairies put love-juice in Theseus's and Hippolyta's eyes.    .....

*After you read*

**25** Tell the story of *Pyramus and Thisby* in as few words as possible.

**26** What do Theseus and Hippolyta think of these? Why?

   **a** the lovers' story       **c** Quince's opening speech

   **b** the actors            **d** the play

**27** Discuss these questions with another student. What do you think?

   **a** What is Puck worried about in his final speech? Why?

   **b** Are dreams important to you? Why (not)?

**Writing**

**28** Imagine that you are Hermia's best friend (in Act 1). You hear about Hermia's plan to run away with Lysander. Is she right to run away, or should she listen to her father? Write her a letter. Give your opinion.

**29** Imagine that you are Lysander (in Act 1). Write a letter to your aunt. Explain why you and Hermia are going to stay with her.

**30** Write about the importance of love-juice in the story. What problems did it make? What problems did it solve?

31 In Act 2 Scene 1, Puck says, 'Oberon smiles at my funny stories. I tell him about all the jokes that I play...' Write one of Puck's funny stories.

32 In Act 4, Bottom wants Peter Quince to write a song called 'Bottom's Dream'. Write the song.

33 Imagine that you are Helena. Write a letter to your father, Nedar. Ask him to come to your wedding with Demetrius. Tell him about your strange night in the wood.

34 Imagine that you are a reporter. Write about *Pyramus and Thisby* for the local newspaper. Was it a good play? Who was the best actor? Who was the worst? What did the audience think of the play? Should your readers go and see it? Why (not)?

35 Describe your favourite person in the play. What do you like about that person?

36 A student magazine has asked readers to write a modern fairy story. The best story will be in the magazine. Write your story.

37 Write about the strangest, funniest or most frightening dream that you can remember. What happened? Who was in it? How did you feel when you woke up? Did the dream mean anything?